PIG JIGS

Written by Nora Gaydos
Illustrated by BB Sams

innovativeKids®

A pig.

A pig and a wig.

A big pig jigs.

A big pig jigs on a hill.

A big pig jigs on a hill and slips.

A big pig jigs on a hill
and slips on a wig.

SLIPS and FLIPS!

A big pig hits his hips.

No jigs!

A big pig sits still on the hill.

After You Read

Answer these questions about the story, and then use words from the story in fun, new ways!

1. What does the pig slip on?
    Why does the pig sit still at the end?

2. What other words rhyme with *pig*?
    What other words rhyme with *hill*?
    What other words rhyme with *sit*?

3. Make up a different sentence of your very own for each of these words: *wig, slip, still.*
    Now try to use all of those words together in *one* sentence!

Skills in This Story

Vowel sound: short *i*
Sight words: *a, and, on, no, the*
Word ending: *-s*
Initial consonant blends: *sl, fl, st*

FISH GIFT

Written by Nora Gaydos
Illustrated by BB Sams

The fish.

The fish lifts.

The fish lifts the gift.

The fish lifts the gift
with its fins.

SNIP, SNIP!

The fish rips the gift.

It is a bib.

The bib fits the fish.

Drip, drip, spill!

The gift is a hit.

After You Read

Answer these questions about the story, and then use words from the story in fun, new ways!

1. What does the fish use to lift the gift?
    Why is the gift a hit?

2. What other words rhyme with *gift*?
    What other words rhyme with *bib*?
    What other words rhyme with *spill*?

3. Make up a different sentence of your very own for each of these words: *fish, rip, snip*.
    Now try to use all of those words together in *one* sentence!

Skills in This Story

Vowel sound: short *i*
Sight words: *the, with, its, is, a*
Word ending: *-s*
Initial consonant blends: *sn, dr, sp*
Final consonant blend: *-ft*
Final consonant digraph: *-sh*